how we eke
A Collection of Poems
Cleo de Nuit

Index

Author's Note   9

Prelude
1. The Sinking Ship   13
2. An Ode to the Stars, Sands, and Each Dying Man   15

Book I
1. To Live   21
2. Stars   22
3. Moon-Kissed   23
4. The Watcher   24
5. The Devil   25
6. The Captain   27
7. Idyll   28
8. Sonnet 5   29
9. Humanity's Hymn   30
10. The Midnight Wind   31
11. Green   32
12. Field of Wheat   33
13. Field of Words   34
14. Well Into The Night   35
15. Mist   36
16. sun song   37
17. Succor   38
18. Script   39
19. The Wondrous   40
20. The Garden   41
21. Matters of Life and Love   42
22. Veracity   43
23. Glow   44
24. Paper   45
25. The Archer's Target   46
26. New Year's   47

27.	At The Lake	48
28.	The Library	49
29.	The Song Of Dawn	50
30.	Frolicking Birds	51
31.	A Tribute to Shakespeare	52
32.	Pink	53
33.	The Dance	54
34.	Bliss	55
35.	Expiation	56
36.	Sincerely, Me	57

Book II

1.	Summer, Winter, Love	59
2.	The Heist of Hearts	60
3.	Of Love and of Hope	61
4.	Strange Room	62
5.	The Waltz of Fall	63
6.	The King	64
7.	The Artist's Tale	65
8.	Wine	66
9.	Marie	67
10.	Day and Dusk	68
11.	Villanelle II	69
12.	The Beach	70
13.	Flee	71
14.	Thicket of Trees	72
15.	The Flow of Time	74
16.	Soliloquy I	75
17.	Romantic Woes	76
18.	Fool	77
19.	The Swings	78

Book III

1. Villanelle III — 82
2. The Night — 83
3. Eros — 84
4. Haunt — 86
5. Shades of Red — 87
6. Knives — 88
7. Love and Lamenting — 89
8. A Long Night — 90
9. Papercut — 91
10. A Somber Survey of My Life — 92
11. Sunslinger — 93
12. Sonnet IX — 94
13. Beyond the Night — 95
14. Warriors — 96
15. The Spider — 97
16. Barren — 99
17. The Rime of Wrath — 100

Book IV

1. To Die — 103
2. Candlelight — 104
3. The Wildflower — 105
4. Blossoming Death — 106
5. Clouds — 107
6. Blue — 108
7. Rue — 109
8. Orpheus — 110
9. The Day — 111
10. The Call To Leave — 112
11. Unlikely Lover — 113
12. In Perdition — 114

13. Another Dying Man	115
14. The Dance of Life	116
15. Titans	117
16. The Widow	119
17. The Soldier	120
18. The Butterfly	122
19. Moments	123
20. The Flower	124
21. Mediocrity	125
22. Ink and Quills	126
23. As I Lie Bleeding	127
24. The House	129
25. The Boy Who Died	130
26. The Funeral	132
Free Space	*136*

Author's Note

I begin this note with a word of gratitude. To you, who I couldn't thank enough for reading, and to everyone else who has shown me support and encouragement. I owe this largely to you.

What can you expect from this book? On unearthing this question, we arrive at another: what, truly, is this book? If I were to describe it in brief, I would call it a 15-year old's musings on what he calls life. I would call it a plethora of realizations, of knowledge gained, and of perspectives swayed by the blow of time. The teens are turbulent years, and I make no attempt to veil that; instead, I embrace it, and try to trap some essence of these years in ink and page.

Life is a collection of fragments and shards. They're sometimes serrated, and sometimes smooth. We spend our lives piecing these fragments together, but seldom can figure out what to make of that we see. Through my poems, I've tried to limn what I've pieced together in words—rhyming lines, metered lines, alliteration, enjambment, the ilk. In publishing this book, I share my fragments and shards with you.

The poems in this book are divided into four portions: "We Dream", "We Try", "We Drudge", and "We Die" (with the exception of the first two poems, which, rather, explore all of these themes). The first section relates to the dreams we develop in youth, a time of solace and bliss. We are, then, like flowers that have just blossomed and do not know what it is to wither. The next section is associated with our attempts at bringing these dreams into reality, and the wavering of the hope of our youth. "We

Drudge" talks of the death of hope, and of the transformation of an ardent existence into a struggle to stay alive. Finally, we read of death, and how we may either accept it or attempt to delay it.

Of course, what I intend to convey may not be what you interpret. That, after all, is the basis of art. It is our ability to relate to art and form our own conclusions, that makes it thrive. I am, thus, extremely enthralled by the prospect of you forming your own interpretations. My words are not tethered to these pages, but merely hosted by them, and I hope that they find a berth in your heart, too!

I hope to one day look past, after plodding past the scorching days of the years to come, and feel glad that I published this book. I do not expect for this book to achieve fame, or even be known by more than a handful. Rather, I hope it is the first step in a journey I shall grow to love. After all, if one is to cross the ocean, they shall need at least a ferry. Let this be the first strip of wood in the ferry that will take me across the seas. Regardless of whether I'm known for my leagues in the ocean or not, I will have have crossed the waters. That is all I dream to do.

I worry I've gotten carried away, and so put a stop to my maundering. I, again, express sincere gratitude, and with great joy present to you (trumpets, please!) "How We Eke", a collection of 100 poems.

Regards,
Cleo de Nuit :)

Prelude
The Sinking Ship

The Sinking Ship
The Life of Hope

We are riding a ship towards the dawn,
Raising the sails and the rusting anchor,
We'll leave the night behind us, going on;

We're no longer tired, our languor is gone,
Not drunken, we're all sober and wiser,
We are riding a ship towards the dawn;

This is surcease to the shadows' sojourn,
The moon grows distant and the sun closer,
We'll leave the night behind us, going on;

The grasp of the dark will leave us alone,
The waking sky rich with motley wonder,
We are riding a ship towards the dawn;

The shroud of the sky is by the sun torn,
The brightness has come, our grief is over,
We'll leave the night behind us, going on!

I now feel hope in this life that's my own,
I can feel joy, perhaps seek a lover,
We are riding a ship towards the dawn,
We'll leave the night behind us, going on;

"This is to live, my dear women, dear men,
We ride the tides, high and low, to the dawn,
An era of grandeur will now begin,

Our hopelessness will soon be fully gone!" ♡

But, then, as I called these very words out,
Our ship, teeming with hope, begins to sway,
A sense of shock and pain has come about,
Are we, after our glee, to be astray?

Our good spirits are lost to the seas blue,
The sky, also blue, just surveys the scene,
The sky, the sea, the day, all of it's blue;

Now all we feel is an embarrassed rue,
We had all been fools in feeling so keen,
Our good spirits are lost to the seas blue,

We glance at each other, "what will we do?"
Even the sun is not as it had been,
The sky, the sea, the day, all of it's blue;

That hope we all then felt was something new,
And a short-lived dream is all it had been,
Our good spirits are lost to the seas blue;

The ship will sink, and with it we will, too,
All I wish to see now's a field of green,
The sky, the sea, the day, all of it's blue;

Is this the end, past all that we've been through?
Are we to just die, by none heard or seen?
Our good spirits are lost to the seas blue,
The sky, the sea, that day, all of its blue.

An Ode to the Stars, Sands, and Each Dying Man

Would you look above at the silk of the sky?
There, a plethora of stars mottle the dark,
They're bright, you may catch them in your eye,
They're scattered, but every inch of the night mark;

They're like a carafe filled to the brim,
With light that they're eager to share,
They're not like the sun, acting on whim,
They beam and emanate a sense of care;

Do you wish you could rise to that height?
Leave the grass and soil behind?
Do you want to touch them, caress their might?
I don't think I would in the slightest mind;

I want to rise to their white candor,
Let me to their white candor rise,
I want to rise, and their power adore,
Let me adore their power and rise;

To rise to the stars I cry and demand,
But I can't reach, I testify I tried!
Instead, I'm tethered to this sand,
To lands beneath which the dead are buried;

I'm tied to the ground on which I'm born,
Under which I'll lie when I die,
Under, when my conscience is gone,
Underneath the soil I'll lie;

Are dreamers all that we are, we?

I cannot leave this world for a star,
Soon, they'll my body in the land bury,
They'll let us soar, but never too far;

Is that the tale of every dead man?
We see all of our endeavors fail,
Throughout our lives told what we can,
We try until our bones grow frail;

Was that the fate of every dead woman?
To drudge until she succumbed to pain?
To squander time until her skin turned wan?
To see in death that all was in vain?

Is that the nature of the life of every person?
To foster hope, and douse it at its peak?
Work as you can! You're tired? You're done!
To taste destitution, grow oblivious and weak?

If so, dear stars, please rain down your light,
We cannot, not ever, rise to your height,
Instead, come down yourself if you might,
Unless you too against the darkness must fight;

Rain your light upon us, my stars,
At least let me have you in my eyes,
In these drab times, don't leave, dear stars!
In hope continue to decorate the skies;

Rain your light upon us all,
For in your light is hope, though brief,
Thus, let it to these harsh lands fall,
The world around is a cruel thief;

Fall, light, without surcease,
And delude us all, beguile us all,
Won't you help us, won't you please?
Rain upon us, we'll watch you fall.

Book I
We Dream

To Live

What, truly, is it to live?
Is it to garner money and gold?
To work and have to try to survive?
To die alone at an age of old?

I wish to live a life of passion,
Of knowledge, and of love,
Even if that means I have to my meals ration,
Because then I will have lived a life I can love.

Stars

We lie beneath
A sea of stars
Two souls coinciding for good;
Your lip is the brightest of berries,
Rich red against the wan of your skin,
And your eyes are grand,
Greater than these skies;
If you were a constellation,
If any star could surmount to your beauty,
I would be an astronomer
And my gaze wouldn't stray from your light.

Moon-Kissed

The moon heralds dark heaven's rise,
In envy vied by the sun's red eyes;
Fiery flames of hell had harrowed,
The seconds that the moon hadn't hallowed;

In the sunshine wheat fields are plowed,
But the moon amuses a lover's plod,
Scorching be the seconds of sunlight,
But the squalor of day drowns in the night;

As moon-deer drone past Helios' horses,
Killing the heat, surcease to my dirges,
Moon-kissed, moon-kissed, moon-kissed, I cry,
Moon kissed be soils wet and dry.

The Watcher

A vampire, probably
The watcher writhes
In the leave of lights,
A ghoul in the sunless sky,
He's sanguine in the moonlight sly;
Nay, none know one so nimble,
His shadows stray where a stone won't stumble,
Lither than the western winds,
He sways where the brightness ends;
In the darkness swims his sorrow sight,
Thirsty for the scent of plight,
Stealing souls in the swell of night,
He's, for a mortal, a violent fright.

The Devil

Tenebrous be the time, and by
The eking light skies vaunt, we glide,
On the seas of brightness dry,
Into the holy dark we ride;
On we roll on the turbid tides,
The mist around a morbid sight,
To dread we deign, for the midnight hides
Many a secret in the lack of light;
Will we sink, or will we summon
Some surreptitious valor veiled,
Will our superstitions have won
Our sanity? We thought as we sailed;
Blanched as the moon we paled,
As by us the floorboards creaked,
Our hearts and soul the terror impaled,
For our blood the shadows lusted!
Oh we knew, oh we knew,
That we were not alone,
Still we stood, surrounded by blue,
Frozen but not alone;
With fear we were stupid and sore,
In none of us any vestige of gall,
For the wind's wild gamboling bore,
That they and we the devil call;
We saw of love, and the life we led,
Frail were we as we said farewell,
For all of us could see ahead,
The axe of Death that shall us fell;
Every man, he fell by day,

And as he crashes down he cries
To God, "save me if you may",
But from the wood not a man did rise,
I was lone, by the break of dawn;
I was lone, as they were blanketed by flies,
Stunned and of rue, I was alone;
In time I saw the bliss of shore,
And kneeling on the Earth,
I told of that my vessel bore,
To douse the island's excited hearth,
They look now at me with pain,
A soldier who has known life's bane,
But their pity be in vain,
For the real truth they have not gained,
That those they'd in their coffins lain,
We're killed by no devil, their prayers too were vain,
They were, no, but another slain,
One that's none but their own captain.

The Captain

Another captain, another sea
Oh you talk of a captain,
Your captain, "god of seas",
But have you heard of our captain?
He's Odysseus in spirit, indeed;

He veers through waters of tales and tyrants,
Singing the shanties of sea;
He touches the mists of myths and fables,
And valor his nickname be;

Of Poseidon's sons and Apollo's aim,
No man be as bright as he,
And of love and life he verses deep,
As of squids and swords;

As our ship drags into the night,
Our sails waving to the breeze,
The feel of fear we know not,
As the captain takes the wheel.

Idyll

Salt of my seas, beat of my heart,
Of love for you my soul may part,
Awake in a lake, a reverie of you;
Tear in my eyes, dew in my skies,
Many a man for your stare vies,
Poets, and lords, and bards just for you;
Soughing through shores, strong in my sails,
Our fable through all the nullity wails,
Glowing and blowing through beaches for you;
Yield of my field, banisher of blue,
Mollify this desire that I brew,
This love is mine, coveting you.

Sonnet 5

No, they're not in order
Is my love by time's tide taken afar,
Or is it still a corpse, stowed in my mind,
Oh, does the pierce of hours my desire mar,
Will you ever the bliss of the truth find?
In the heat of the sun my passion seethes,
Shall pass of days wean me of need for you?
Oh merely, barely, my skin my lust sheaths,
At the curve of your lips it's born anew;
I rue the time spent away from your sight,
In my eyes it is none but all squandered,
As for Helen's love was great war and fight,
For you from no turmoil may I wander;
In garish seas of seconds did I drown,
But you have raided the gloom from this town.

Humanity's Hymn

Alone I eke in this frenetic city,
Somber I stray, in me a fight,
But merry I stay, amidst the light,
Revering the grace of humanity;
In the gardens I see a baby's glee,
And in my sleep I feel jovial bliss;
As your eternal amour I miss,
I sing a song for humanity;
On a stroll, I see our felicity,
And beam at one's love serene,
Together, we long a world pristine,
And utter a pledge, for humanity;
Oh, how a kiss can turn one giddy,
And how another can soothe a scare,
I sigh at how well we fare,
Writing this letter to humanity

The Midnight Wind

I dance to the rhythm of your whispers,
A march to the manic of your pulse,
The echo of your breath in a silent room,
Shall be limned in a thousand ballads;
I take your hand, an arrow of stars,
The moon and sun's diverging bright,
And as time jogs past the light,
We waltz to the midnight wind.

Green

a scene of green
a sea of trees
a labyrinth of bushes
a cult of birds

a ferry of rock
a path of tar
a forest of flowers
a plethora of plants

the scene swayed
to the speedy wind
and waves rushed
in the ocean of green

Field of Wheat

The wind whistles its way
Through the field of wheat,
We whisper songs of love
Wafted away by the flowing air;
The day shall give way to the night sky,
Holding the moon up with pride,
The breath of the wind shall see surcease,
And these soils shall grow too chilly to stand on,
But, forever, our love shall linger on,
In the wake of which the wheat shall grow,
That which shall keep the sun's warmth alive.

Field of Words

Give me all of your words, oh, men!
I shall harvest them in my field,
And when they grow, you ask, what then?
Then, you'll taste what the land will yield;

Let my fields spread, I dearly plead,
Let these words embrace our cold world,
With the words shall the people be fed,
And with knowledge, they shall be bold;

Let us our blades and wrath eschew,
And in this reign of words all live,
Let us all be reborn, anew,
And in these fields of words we'll thrive.

Well Into The Night

I sought you in an unholy hour,
As a carafe carried the silk of night,
Enigma yours held a blasphemous power,
From the somber seas a tranquil might;
On the midnight dew I'm delightfully drunk,
Maundering the shadows' ramble;
Into your eye, the moon, I'm sunk,
Passing but death's own amble;
Tenebrous tales plod on these roads,
Witches, and potions with toads;
Roaming the nights be the devil's own hordes,
Bellowing in the billowing wind unholy words;
Yet past the sun's seamless scorn,
Be the penance of time,
When garishness sleeps, and stars skies adorn,
Hymned be the quiet's own rime.

Mist

Your welcome mist hangs
Over my solitary thicket of trees,
And in the rain that shall soon fall
I shall thrive, I shall flourish,
In these drops of silver youth,
Is nimbleness I haven't hitherto seen,
Pink are the flowers now, hither,
I was sure they would soon wither!
Trickling down my bark, my body,
Is amour beyond what many may fathom,
The mist, the rain, drops of life,
Are all the epitome of youthful love.

sun song

I wrote this during a geography lesson
Sulking like a shadow,
I am a shade in your sun;
But sitting under the willow,
You tell me I'm the one;
Alone in yonder meadow,
My love your had won,
You shine upon the morrow,
The last vestige of fun;
So kiss me as our love you sow,
With lips softer none,
And do it as you fill my hollow
Tethering time's run.

Succor

I ramble the songs we sang,
And murmur the poems we wrote,
In daydreams I long to feel
The perennial warmth of your skin;

I yearn the feel your tender lips,
To bungee deep into your eyes,
As our bodies reconcile,
Does my soul greatly rejoice;

Your maundering matters,
I will recite your words by day,
For you are a fire that placates
The crippling chill of my mind.

Script

In these seas of salt
No rock I shall cling to
But yours, smooth and firm;
My eyes burn to learn
The hallowed chapters of your past
And I long to study and cherish
Your life's sacred script.

The Wondrous

Let us go on snow gilded flight,
Through these villages bright,
For they're heaven on land of earth,
Of songs sung around hot hearth,

In the dripping window's blur,
With coffee before storms occur,
Are days so grand and merry,
That we find ourselves jocular, very;

Such are the delights of men,
At such sights to beam we begin,
And despite the chill in the air,
Our spirits shall stay rather fair.

The Garden

In these gardens you find,
Tulips, the caress of spring and kiss of bliss,
With youth you'd mustered in the years that went amiss;
Past the wisteria, you find,
A gate of iron, dull with age,
It whinges as it swings in rage;
Tumultuous above, the skies you find,
The sun veiled by the hue of night,
Above, there is now barely any light;
In the trees you find,
A sparrow's nest, with whinging babies to show,
With innocent eyes, careless groans,
And a dream to nurture and sow;
You were, too, once such a bird,
Once like a tulip, once young,
Now you're rusty, as that gate you saw,
Or as the sky, shrouded by the dark.

Matters of Life and Love

Your beauty heals pestilence,
And the light does not dare cross your path,
Your glow to beat a candle in the dark;
The earth roars at you,
In tones of reverence,
And in the heat of the sun,
Your beauty is the cool wind;
We hold to our heart
An almost regal love-
A desire to relish,
Blossoming flowers
On hills high and low.

Veracity

I will taste on my tongue
The dew that falls from the sky,
For raging above is a storm:
The tempest of our love;
We can't defy this love,
I shan't defy its veracity,
This is the golden verity,
That shan't be concealed,
Our fables have overlapped,
And now they are of love,
I can only hope, as I hold your hand,
That they see a joyous end.

Glow

The moon shall rise,
Only to set again
And a bird's nest it shall,
Inevitably, always flee,
Every seed in a field of wheat,
Shall one day very soon fall;
Yet you can rise, but needn't fall-
And when you do ascend, glow like the sun,
Glow, and I will see you,
I will see you, and I shall so fain,
Even when nobody else will.

Paper

Your cheeks are ruddy, plums of youth,
Your skin is polished by rouge,
As you stand in your gown, so grand,
In me sparks pugnacious passion;
Leave your love in ink, on paper,
For I can't cherish all of you now,
And God forbid my haste snatches
Some of your grandeur.

The Archer's Target

I am an archer, my fingers are sly,
But my heart was until now dry,
Now, I have seen you and your love,
And to desire you I'm behoved,
Your love is my archer's target,
And my passion is the bow I nock.

New Year's

2021

Cheers erupt as the clock strikes midnight,
This night, and the dawn to follow,
Shall both be redolent with hope;
On the morrow, past sunrise,
The dew that rains shall be no sweeter,
Yet the end of an year and start of another,
Sees in us the rebirth of dreams,
May this time, we fare a bit better,
Beam a bit more and live a life of love.

At The Lake

Our fingers intertwine,
And our feet are numb in the chill of the lake-
I gaze up at the stars,
But the heavens know I think of none but you;
Your elegance is limned in the ripples of the lake,
And the moon's light is dim in the wake of your glow,
This memory shall, in perdition, all of my pain soothe;
The wind soughs through the waving trees,
Jauntily shuffling your silky hair:
Golden to the eye, and smooth to touch;
Oh, waves of time, won't you slow for us?
I wish I could for eternity relive this moment-
your sight is worth an eon of admiration.

The Library

This is a world of words,
Tragedies in thin wan sheets,
Wonders in white, and pain on page;
The library stands with trembling might,
Refuge for all with yearning,
With power in its brick and books;
Darling, I give you my word,
That no page of paper shall burn,
As long as I haunt these shelves.

The Song of Dawn

I did on a plod my time all erode,
Treading damp soils of moonlight drunk,
When regiments of yours on light the night rode,
Gnawing the sky that's in shadows sunk;

Blanching the night, you speared it with white,
To stain the pale sheet of all that above,
The swords of your men did banish the night,
A blissful lay you that day wove;

You limned the sky in the richest dye,
Rising from seas of peace unknown,
You then watched as the darkness died,
A garden of red had then above you grown;

The hegemony of dark has seen now surcease,
The moon's empire is now in debris,
For brief a time, he did your rise see,
I stare at you as you rise above me.

May my love I in such beauty paint?
Yellow, and mellow, your passion is flame,
The skies you so easily gained,
May my desire to grandeur I tame?

Frolicking Birds

I see above a frolicking bird,
And just behind it a second, a third,
They chirr as they mottle the sky,
The wind soughs with them as they cry,

The birds then vanish, leaving the sky plain,
And soon even the blue from the sky drains,
It's dark now, birds, and I miss you,
I miss your play, birds, and the blue sky too.

A Tribute to Shakespeare

Desire yours ebbs in ink of black and blue,
To quench our hearts, as in passion we bathe,
Of life and love, grief, Rome, Venice and rue,
In words did you limn lores of wist and wrath;
You were a man, indeed were one a man,
Merely but that? Nay, you were a lot more,
Pathos and pain contained in parchment wan,
Of my wonder and love I'm some times sore;
Suave you were, in words a jest or jeer,
You dropped down your blade and picked up your quill,
Shakespeare, with tales of love and them of fear,
With your stories and songs did you lands till;
Upon our fields wry your tempest arrived,
And with mere words did you bring us alive.

Pink

Villanelle I

Pink is the dawn in which stars sink,
And berries in a wind-washed field,
Your rouge, your lips, your love, all pink;

The sky is cleaned of the night's ink,
The clouds us from the sun's might shield,
Pink is the dawn in which stars sink;

Yet, warmer is your tender wink,
And light to which I may well yield,
Your rouge, your lips, your love, all pink;

I stand, amidst the wind's nimble jink,
And look at what has our day sealed,
Pink is the dawn in which stars sink,

You are the better dawn I think,
For your love may not wane or kneel,
Your rouge, your lips, your love, all pink;

As the sun wields light in skies pink,
It is your love that I do wield,
Pink is the dawn in which stars sink,
Your rouge, your lips, your love, all pink.

The Dance

This was one of my earliest poems(:
And we were swaying,
Your hands on mine,
Your touch bringing not just warmth,
But surges of glee;

Your eyes shine,
Ablaze with pink fire,
Is it really us dancing,
Or is the floor sinuously swinging?

The grace we radiate attract eyes,
They can try to make us stop-
But, no, not even the chains
of Thanatos could bind us;

 I could fall to my death,
But my eyes still wouldn't stray from your face,
And your beauty shall resurrect me.

Bliss

Bliss is your eyes with its lustrous tint,
Perfume on your skirt, vanilla's hint,
Enticing as a god's usher,
You make gardens lusher;
Wine-red: your lips as you close the air,
Wind-lithe: my fingers through the sleek of your hair,
The goddess of hearth felt pensive in your leave,
No flame is as incandescent as the breaths you heave;
And tonight, we're a prince and a witch,
Audacious, we're dancing on a bridge:
The link of heaven and hell,
We're swimming with seas to dwell.

Expiation

The buds of hope may blossom past the paring January chill,
But the dying tulip sees not beyond the eternal night;
The pacing peasant pities the crop the winters kill,
He smiles but at the notion of the sparing spring's light;
Zephyr, soughing, sighs at the surfeit of suffering seen,
Breathing will's might into the failing bird's trill,
Knowing, nevertheless, that come shall safety's sheen;
The numbing baby's cry, now piercing skies so shrill,
Shall fade to fondling smiles at the thought of what had been,
And the soils that gave him dirt he shall have grown to till;
The flower's frost fades with the attrition of the cold,
And its tale be told with newfound youth's elation,
For the drab of bleak December into life's love shall mold,
And in the chaste dawn's sight be warm expiation.

Sincerely, Me

I wrote this for my crush at 12?
Her eyes are tame but raging oceans,
Where I could drift for long
In my old oak cockleshell;
Her hair is a swaying dash of gold,
Of fall leaves and caramel-
Before her, my heart has never failed to flutter;
Her fierce, valiant nature,
Her warm ways,
Of the laughs we've had,
And the tint on my cheeks at times,
My love for her's never wavered.

xxx

Book II
We Try

Summer, Winter, Love

Another sonnet! I wrote most of this
one walking around a mall-I
must have looked quite eccentric.

The fresh year's blade be bearing blood of love,
Of lancing hearts of men gay, young, and bold,
In March twine hands beneath the sunshine's stove,
And April hymns of beams to kill the cold;
In May taints air the scent of spring's desire,
The streets of summer teem with amour's maids,
August be warm, but their souls foster fire,
And no worse in the winter months one fares;
Fall leaves be dry, but sweet be lay of theirs,
Skies cloudy shall never douse the flames galore,
Succor of love the shroud of winter pares,
In late December snow, to stars surmounts amour;
Bestows time in us both joy and pain,
I wait for days it shall show me my fain.

The Heist of Hearts

My maundering is meek in your light,
In your floral grace and your moonlit might,
You found me an archer's target,
And your arrow struck my soul;

Into the nocturnal wind we whisper,
A swaying song of beauty and battle,
A sweet hymn to honor a sweeter love,
Love that shall clear drudgery, dust and smoke;

Of starry nights and lecherous fights,
Of worried glances and confused kisses,
You were a thief in the wildest of nights,
And I lost myself to your heist of hearts.

Of Love and of Hope

Of all the eroded roads I've taken,
None have I roamed beside an other man,
But now I'm by your love held and shaken,
And when it bloomed, a new epoch began;
My dear, we roamed on here a lonely ilk,
My heart was weak, beating a mellow waltz,
But when I touch your skin, as soft as silk,
That doused fire in my soul's hearth sparks and rolls;
Are you to end this mellow melody?
Or just more to limn in my rueful rime?
Under your warm sun blossoms life in me,
Will you bring joy after the sorrow's time?
In years of mine, I never light ahead had seen,
Will you me pardon hope that waits glee's sheen?

Strange Room

In a rather strange room I pace,
The air is sour, the floor is cold,
The scent is fusty, my eyes burn,
Around the wretched room I went;

In a rather strange room I pace,
It is at least a decade old,
Of chagrin my spirits now churn,
And for this I have to pay rent!

In my hands is buried my face,
The air is sour, the floor is cold,
A man once died in here, I learn,
I would rather live in a tent;

The state I'm in is of disgrace,
The strange room reeks badly of mold,
The scent is fusty, my eyes burn,
Will these terrible days never end?

Seems not, for even now I pace,
One more day, in a grunt I'm told,
I wish, now, only to return,
Around the wretched room I went.

The Waltz of Fall

Bow before me, mortal meddlers,
For the sacred waltzer of autumn I be,
My bark hosts the race of dew,
And with cries of my golden girth,
We whoop the whimsical wind;
From my shedding leaves, with a chirr a bird soars,
At its fearless flight you stare,
My leaves are motley, frolicking with Zephyr,
And my roots deep in the docile soil;
The glee of fall has set into the world,
Soon, but, shall the winter's stabbing cold come,
Soon shall, in the wake of ice, a sojourn of suffering start,
And I shall be just, merely, another tree,
Bare and vulnerable and stripped of my might.

The King

Casque of good gold, he calls himself king,
Carafes of blood to vaunt each new kill,
But truly, tis a queen of whom we all sing,
Of her of all soils and rivers that rill;
Spear of sharp iron, he calls himself brave,
Wields he a sword drunk on ichor,
But we call them daring the peasants who save
Us all from hunger, in them is true valor,
They call a soldier he who the cruel wars fought,
But we see a soldier in the breeze of the water
In wry drought, the one of wars can save us not,
But a lake of blue love, to us it shall cater,
None be as rich as the soil he was born on,
And no man be king of the ground he never won.

The Artist's Tale

His brush rubs the white,
In silent strokes of suffering,
In grim shades of hopeless gray,
But in garish tones of yellow too;
The artist's sinew swivels,
The world is his sole subject,
His picture is, both, a joyous thing,
And a strikingly somber scene;
The canvas is a fiasco of paint,
In it captured just a mere inkling
Of the world's ceaseless chaos-
The same that we all toy and gambol by,
And also that we drudge and flounder in.

Wine

I don't drink, should I really be writing about wine?
Our love is wine to wake in me passion,
Blood-red in the banal gray days I eke,
In the night's chill I was before ashen,
But now I may your fire in winter seek;
Of this succor my flesh does ache and heat,
Will you my time all waste and mind litter?
The scarlet dew, on my open lips sweet,
Now in my mouth does turn a bit bitter;
You cloy my tongue, for my vanity you kill,
You burn my throat, as a desire you brew,
You haunt my sleep, and I some times am ill,
Starstruck I shall but love for ever you;
Dear one, I am direly on this love drunk!
Of love for you I am very much drunk.

Marie

The glory of gales before Marie's skin pales,
No lass can fain to dance quadrilles so deft,
And dear, to stir a heart she never can fail,
Her cheeks warmer than her love you left;
Marie's blue eyes are bright, robust with light,
Alas, vies but your heart for someone else;
In sorrow your professed desire last night,
So she in sleep hers dreams of wedding bells;
Caressing her hair, her gloom you do fear,
But you yearn in your mind the one you want,
And so Marie you flee, to lands not near,
Killing that hers that once she could flaunt;
Marie old grows, and dies with her back sore,
But never lived she happy after twenty-four.

Day and Dusk

Third sonnet in a row? I promise you the next few are lighter.
May I call you the summer morrow's sun?
Your welcome rise brings forth a graceful day,
From your shine other stars cower and run,
But will I in your warmth die and decay?
I feel in you, too, the cool quiet solace
Of dusk, to vie the might the sun invites,
You bring the breeze much yearned after hot days,
But will I freeze in the chill of your nights?
I feel you are none, but that crack of time,
Before the hours of day the stars take away,
The moon, it mourns, as light echoes its rime,
The night cascades, and the sky wears a gray;
Between the war of dusk and day be peace,
Oh, that are you, of heaven one a piece.

Villanelle II

Team dusk?
The light is dead, the day departs,
Oh! Of its garish bright we're free,
Fare well! For a new reign now starts,

The last of rubble we roll on carts,
The birds frolic and insects flee,
The light is dead, the day departs,

We now caress our aching hearts,
May some solace our gray souls see,
Fare well! For a new reign now starts,

Oh, so mellow beneath the stars,
Languid in the darkness we be,
The light is dead, the day departs,

Before you my veneer now parts,
Right now I feel your love in me,
Fare well! For a new reign now starts,

The heat no more may pare my heart,
No, now creatures of love are we,
The light is dead, the day departs,
Farewell! For a new reign now starts.

The Beach

Delayed at dusk, in sorrow I sat,
Upon the cool and hapless sand,
The coffers of my heart of sadness were fat,
By me blue tides were gnawing on land;
A nimble new wave then on my skin spat,
And the cold it drew forth long later still strays,
I silently for a bit longer on the beach sat,
They were tranquil at night, too hot at day;
I felt some of my turmoil then vanish,
My mind had just now been in anguish,
Now I feel just oblivion and languish,
Somnolence come, I fell asleep by the corniche.

Flee

Our love is the dawn of succor,
But it is shunned aside by the jealous sun,
It is a star in the shy night sky,
Hidden but by the moon's keen shine,
Your words frame the story of my life,
And you are the light I see the world with,
So let us, my darling, run far away,
To where our love may fill the skies.

Thicket of Trees

I remember, one summer, I felt like a seer,
The tides of my time were toyed by my moon,
I could see it all, each epoch, every year,
Mottled with grandeur that would come soon;
My life, sprawled before me, was for once clear,
And my room, my town felt too dingy for me;
The roads were all plain and the silence stifling,
The skies were smirking and the people were nosy,
To leave it all behind in me was a longing;
That summer I rode a bicycle, was it cozy!
And passed on most days the same thicket of trees,
I turned each time that past it I drove,
Unruly succor is all in it one sees,
Rich was the verdure of that vehement grove,
Alive with cadence of crickets and hum of bees,
A sight to stain my soul with love!
And I recall that one tree stood short with a stoop,
Most of the times I did at it stare,
It did stand out in the glamorous group,
It's bark was dry, feeble, and bare,
And it's branches in a mellowly droop;
I then wondered if I'd any better than that fare?
For I could see many a man in that tree,
Wry with worry and muffled by strain,
I may just like that tree soon be,
Losing my leaves and taunted by rain,
I could be just like those men I do see,
In resigned languor, to do nothing fain;
No, I may not to such life acquiesce,

I must strive, vie for the light,
May not my ardor and advance ever cease,
Even against the attrition of plight;
May I be the tallest tree, please?
For that reign I shall indeed fight,
Fie the grass that's overgrown and grimy,
And the chill that does my being pare,
Fie the ones that may me stall only,
Tripping me with insincere care,
And fie these lands that I eke, lonely,
For it could never my fruit truly bear;
Yet will I miss these people, their nature?
They are all I've known, and all I've lived off,
Will I feel remorse for these moments as I mature?
My lancing loathing, each sarcastic scoff?
Will, in the wake of my ambition, my loves all rupture?
They are, after all, all I've known of;
So clear before, it no more seems certain,
Nothing, no more, what am I to do?
My life ahead seemed veiled by some curtain,
A shroud of doubt, of worry, what will I do?
Will I miss what I lose, loathe what I gain?
And, oh, what is it truly that I'm headed to?

The Flow of Time

The flowers fall, and the fruits ripen,
As the snake sheds its skin, and again,
As the moon's rise stifles the sun;
The wind changes its speed and path,
Just as the ways of the world are changed,
Just as we change, and grow, and forget,
Just as we love, and lose that we love;
So can I compare time to a flowing river?
The current cool and fast, its run ever-changing?
If so, then, as you swim in this river,
You learn more, and earn more too,
But never again shall you see,
The fish you saw along the way,
Along, when you were younger, stronger.

Soliloquy I

I'm sorry, that's the only name I could think of
On my stone your blade is whet,
Upon my shadow your knife of light,
Will I ever your attention get?
Or will I always plod in plight?
Will my love fuel this great eclipse?
Or will I still trudge in turmoil?
I fall prey to your love, your lips,
Will you any of my hopes foil?
And do I truly feel concern?
Or is it just my fear to love?
Must I at your giggles turn stern?
I do, at least, you fondness owe,
Alas, let this grand game go on,
Oh, I am now caught in your gaze,
Despite lather and blood, go on,
For you do not me fail to daze.

Romantic Woes

I really do need to learn to move on better
You wear your sadness like a fleece,
Your blood is sour, flowing cerise,
From every wound it runs on,
Dry on skin like rust on iron;
Each day you feel the strike of rue,
The sky is gray, your minutes blue,
The grip of grief each second grows,
All's dreary with romantic woes.

Fool

Your flames, a blend of scarlet and gold,
Has candor and coveting to make metal molt,
But to burn, my heart doesn't need your fire,
Your mere sight can set it ablaze;
Yet, I'm only a dusty, fusty glove,
That shall your painted nails conceal,
Just a veil to hide your face and grace,
So let me my coveting cease;
How could an aberrant fool as me,
Muster to love you the temerity?
What could one ever in me see?
None, nothing, so how could we be?

The Swings

I swing from skies to soil and sands,
Oh, high above and down below!
As the world rolls beneath my hands,
My weight into the air I throw;

The world so banal as I amble,
Now roars in love and rage anew,
The birds all chirr and men all ramble,
And I no longer see just blue;

Below a tree of birch I be,
From ground to gray above I go,
I swing, I swing, I swing with glee,
But will my hands of pain let go?

Oh no, I say, may not I slip,
And hit that land so firm below,
But aches and pains me plague, I slip,
I slip and hit the ground below;

Then I fall, and I fall, again,
From high, a height of hope and joy,
I crawl, I crawl on dirt again,
The ground I'm on my nostrils cloy;

I fall, in pain I fall again,
All is dull, all that I see,
I watch all of that solace drain,

Will as happy I again be?

I fall, I fall, and fall again,
Off the swings on that tree of birch,
The world once bright is bleak again,
And I just stand alone and watch.

xxx

Book III
We Drudge

*time speeds up as you grow older-
or maybe, you just take things slower,
and time leaves you behind*

Villanelle III

My skin is wan, the skies are wry,
Why is the winter so amiss?
My day is gray and so am I.

My hair is mussed, my lips are dry,
Oh, won't you them please stroke and kiss?
My skin is wan, the skies are wry.

Oh, I beneath the clouds do lie,
Dark clouds! They are in somber bliss,
My day is gray, and so am I.

I stare up, and the air I fie!
Alas! The summer's joy I miss,
My skin is wan, the skies are wry.

Oh, look! This bland day soon will die!
The night shall be better than this!
My day is gray, and so am I.

I wait, I dream, I hope, I cry,
Oh, may the moon this pain dismiss!
My skin is wan, the skies are wry,
My day is gray, and so am I.

The Night

This is also an earlier poem-I suppose you can tell.
We flee, now, into the night,
When the stars puncture the skies,
When envious clouds plead for a glance,
And even the air is heavy with darkness;

Like an audacious owl we venture,
Chivalrous, as the shadows advance,
We hear a rustle, a whisper, a crack,
Is it a ghost? Or merely a crow?

What we are, and what we do,
Shall be hidden by the reticent night,
To be known by only the beings of the dark-
they are the outcasts during day;

We are a secret kept safe by the night.

Eros

In youth you were a fleeting love,
A dream that never would be real,
A flower in my wilting grove,
I lost you in time's turbid reel;

You were, later, a lancing love,
To reign my days and haunt my nights,
Of whim, a stormy, sultry love,
Of succor, passion, oh, and might,

Now, grown, you are a tranquil love,
Penance, peace, past drudging desire,
This sacred idyll be limned in love,
In chill of dusk a graceful fire;

This love has fought the tides of life,
From yonder youth, our naive time,
To this serene epoch, past strife,
And to this love I pen this rime;

Oh, now, I see the dawn of hope,
And you to me the light herald,
In you I feel the heat of hope,
In days of calm and nights ribald,

So bathe me in this crimson light,
Of gold this holy love is wrought,
I shall for this for ever fight,
Oh, this is all I've ever sought!

Thus when the dusk does, nimble, arrive,
When I my soul to death bequeath,
Even then our amour shall thrive,
This love shall be my shroud at death.

Haunt

In time, I hoped I would forget of you,
That you'd be no more than a yonder rue,
But I still do flounder in a great blue,
I still yearn and covet, still do for you;
As a corpse's stench in the air it vaunts,
Our love, rotten now, still my tired mind haunts,
Despite the truism that it is dry and gaunt,
Despite that no body that love still wants;
So now I cry to you one final plea,
Can we our love in the black soil bury?
Otherwise, this love shall for ever be,
A lost, moody love that will never flee.

Shades of Red

Red is the blood that keeps me alive,
And the sun that wakes me daily,
It is the wine that lets nights thrive,
And signals on the streets I see;

But to it's not the blood that drips
It is the red I see on you,
Your rouge is red, so are your lips,
All else, for me, is only blue.

Knives

you bleed a billion cuts,
and grieve with you I would,
but my vapor mustn't
make your clouds pour;

die, oh poison of love!
for every wound you cover
was traced by knives
you once polished;

and to let my wild love flow
in your sinuous, lithe currents,
may make healing bruises blacker,
render your night darker.

Love and Lamenting

In the bitter of our lamenting,
Hides the sweetness of wine,
For in my grief I'm merely tied
Closer and closer to you;

This is pain, that we cannot deny,
But I may find light, for I'm with you,
Like the blood that carries life in us,
May our love shepherd us out of our sorrow.

A Long Night

I restlessly await the rise of your dawn,
For your sun is all that shines upon me,
But tonight, the starts just stray on,
And the darkness that was continues to be,
Your light does not pierce this night,
Your love has now begun to wane,
Yet mine for you has lost no might,
So I shall be the one led to pain.

Paper-cut

A paper-cut stings when penitence seeps,
Remorse in you as the parchment reaps,
In shades of rue your flesh weeps,
Parting your skin as misery leaps;
The joyous souls, they bleed in red,
In rosy ruddiness their chivalry creeps,
But wounds of yours flash melted lead,
Attrition of pain on ghastly skin;
Your soul is the blue of skies overhead,
Your body a loveless effigy of sin,
Yet you walk on the ground your coffin shall fill,
Seldom a loss, seldom a win;
What's left of you is stifled and ill,
Harrowed is your tale, to tell no kin
Waiting and waiting, you drain all your will,
And survey the life you barely are in.

A Somber Survey of My Life

I miss my days of joy and love,
And wow at this mess I've become,
For I plod in just sadness now,
In silent lands I can't call home,
I yearn for my youth and ardor,
For then when I could freely love,
Now in nothing I find succor,
I slowly to my demise row;
All I was proud of's at the pyre,
All before me's a morose lay,
My past I do dearly desire,
That's all I do, every day.

Sunslinger

The gold in the ring you now her bring,
Was once in your eyes, looking at her,
A crown you once wore, but no longer king,
You rust in helplessness, merely a lover;

At seven, they all called you sunslinger,
You dreamt of carriages driving to the sun,
But time robbed that what in you did linger,
And age from you your hallowed youth won.

Sonnet IX

Nope, not in order-sorry:(
In youth we are wild-flowers in the wind,
Dipping, diving, dancing to the day's call,
In our garish petals we all glee find,
Alas, they shall but soon to the soil fall;
Now we all bear fruits, and of it we stoop,
I do not feel the old relief of hope,
My colors have faded, and I always now droop,
I feel the fruit's weight-it'll also soon drop;
And then what is to come, what will then be?
Is this the end, did for just this we drudge?
We grew, we gained, did ever live but we?
Is our life here merely a blot, a smudge?
Was it merely some hasty race to die?
If so, I rue those days bland and gone by.

Beyond The Night

We sting and smite, sanguine, with spite,
Perfidy to the chastity of stars,
But yonder in time shall reign the white,
Past the wrath of the wars;
"Cease! Cease!" the commoner calls,
As his soil by a spear is stained with blood,
But on and on the storm of our rage rolls,
In it's wake misery's flood;
We wound and wield, to no avail,
To vaunt our vanity's might;
But peace, peace, peace shall prevail,
Past the malice of the night.

Warriors

An archer, when he nocks his bows,
Sees not the morrow's frenetic rue;
But as, in memory, on a ferry he rows,
He drowns in a sense of blue;
The swordsman, as his blade he wields,
Longs none but one's blood to draw,
But as he roams ruined fields,
In regret he his blade down throws;
In a steady second of unwavering will,
We take life's ephemeral boon,
And it's not merely another we kill,
But ourselves, our innocence gone too soon;
We'll many a chalice with tears fill,
Just to draw some red that shall dry to maroon.

The Spider

Oh, there! A net, a spider web,
And in it caught a feeble fly,
Flapping, fragile, oh, fie that web!
Alas, it soon shall surely die;

"I, too, am but a fly", I wail!
You are the spiders that bind me,
Tethered I am, in your grasp frail,
A web of white is all I see;

But you yell back, to me you sing,
"We shall save you and you repair"
So bow to that spider, your king,
And well in life shall you, dear, fare,

So stifle your will, your hope, your dreams,
Bury your trifles, and grab a rifle!
"This web is all you have, it seems,
So stay with us, and stay servile."

But oh, why mayn't you leave me be!
And take too your veneers garish,
Scram, go, oh, stray away from me!
To live, to be alone I wish!

May not you drown me with your will,
Or keep me in your stubborn grasp,
You mayn't, not ever, me too kill,
So leave, and lax your ceaseless clasp,

Let me be, please let me go, fly!
I shall bow to no queens or kings,
Let me live, or leave me to die,
Too long stiff have been these two wings;

To leave, and leave for good I plead,
Leave me and I shall leave you too,
Go far and go away, I plead,
Leave for once, and I shall leave you.

Barren

When shall we get some solace, when?
I cannot call this refuge home,
For no field be as barren,
As this loveless land we roam.

The Rime of Wrath

In me does now erupt that flame,
Of wrath, to burn my soul in rage,
This that I fain tend to, not tame,
Does see my peace all rust and age;

As the tempest in clear blue skies,
The roar of wrath, so wry, does vie,
My soul to claim, besmirch, it tries!
A reign of red does by me lie;

The rage does in my blood rampage,
And shred the sweet serene before,
Against the calm it wars do wage,
Alas! Be gone, and stay no more!

But must this rage stall and falter?
For we do burn in heat of time,
Our shrill cries these cruel skies savor,
Silence is bliss, thus yell this rime!

Yes, live on and on with this rage,
For it shall from the world you shield!
It shall, yes, let you free, not cage,
Wield it, and not to their greed yield;

My chagrin's fire be warm in me,
It shan't, indeed, me burn or maim,
The sun of sin scorns what should be,
But anger mine it may not tame;

Cease not, never, your ardent stride,
Against the winds of hate and pride,
No, you must but against it stride,
Pare, prick, and fight, but never hide;

This be a rime of rage, of wrath,
A hymn in hate of hate, in wrath,
A rime, a rime, of rage, of wrath,
A hymn indeed of hate, of wrath.

xxx

Book IV
We Die

To Die

To die is a rather odd deal,
Is it truly even an ordeal?
At worst, there's some pain,
Pain you'll feel never again;

To live is an odder deal,
And this, truly, is an ordeal,
Most of our lives are quite fruitless,
I'd rather die, may I confess?

Candlelight

May I compare our love to the candlelight?
Fierce and keen and burning through the night?
Even against the dark, it remains bright,
And so shall stay against all plague and plight;
In such idyll, I have no pain in me,
Just ceaseless bliss, not an ache, nor trifle,
None may haunt me but your golden beauty,
It's a light no wind nor war will stifle,
I do but fear that I will soon perish,
And what will be of our tale when I do?
For nothing but to be by you I wish,
But my wishes will die with me, is it so?
If love my love for ever I can not,
I shall love until the moment I rot.

The Wildflower

To the song of the wildflower,
Dancing in the thunderstorm,
I waltz with you, rain with you;
To the beat of the butterfly's wings,
In tranquil spring nights,
I sing to you, shelter you;
To the murmur of the seas,
In the sandiest beach,
We swim to the tide,
Followers of the wind;
To the widow's envious eyes,
In the heartiest of coves,
I smile with you, stun with you;
And when the smoke burns high,
When our ash grows dry,
I'll die with you, rot with you.

Blossoming Death

Death has all these years lain dormant,
In patience waiting to lance at my life,
Every time the sun came and went,
It whetted its blade, of bones a knife;
Its time shall very soon arrive,
And I shall acquiesce to peacefully die,
My youth in shreds, I cannot stay alive,
So let my corpse rot and grow dry.

Clouds

I could not take my eyes away
From the lines on the palm of my hand,
They would remain there for eternity,
All I have from the days of my youth;

Now, as I die and head to heaven,
I have little to show from my life below,
Yet as I surveyed the scene before me, unsure,
I felt suddenly docile, in comfort,

Around me were the people I knew,
My kin, my loves, my enemies, all,
I felt not an inkling of anything
But relief, to know I wasn't alone;

We had all sinned, we had all drudged,
We could not refute what we had been,
But here, we did not need to be that,
In this land of clouds could we may seek penance;

So let us be more than lumps of meat,
Of blood, tears, lather, hate, love,
Let us be nothing at all but ourselves,
As in this pleasant land we roam.

Blue

Death is easier to write than life is
The currents frolic around me,
And the fish venture against the tide,
I do not feel the roughened sand,
For my skin is numb, divested of sense;
The sun's rays impale the water,
Only to be shredded by a vengeful current,
The bright star and I,
Are both only spots in the blue;
The sled of life in me did speed,
As did the clamor of my aching heart,
I may be numb, but I could, too, feel
The grasp of life lax around me.

Rue

In sunlight I'm limned,
My ventures all hymned,
But in heaven with rue,
All pales before you.

Orpheus

I sought in you refuge from the world,
And so in your death I'm a destitute,
Beneath the tempests of these skies,
These skies that shroud the heaven you're in;

I waltz alone in the ballroom of the world,
Now empty, deserted, and out of light,
I fancy your face in shadows, spinning,
I'm humming a bleak dirge to you;

You were the stars in my tenebrous skies,
And now I know none but to lament your leave,
All of my days shall be fruitless, vain,
What am I truly, if I'm not yours?

The Day

Beneath the afternoon beams' greeting,
Past the belated breaking of a fast,
I wished I could call it a day;
With beads of sweat in the heat,
Without any spread on my bread,
I longed dearly to call it a day;
At the thickening darkness of dusk,
After the sun's garish sojourn,
I coveted to call it a day;
Now, as I lie away my time,
My last few moments, I surely can say,
I hope to just call it a day,
But only when I'm buried in soil,
With my breathing having found surcease
Shall I be let to call it a day.

The Call to Leave

If all that haunts your dreams are the mistakes of your past,
If all, you feel, is vain, if you see nothing holding hope,
Then, darling, it is time for you to leave at last;
If no man, no thought, no fire may warm the icy storm in you,
If no moment feels bright, and everything's a shade of blue,
Why not just leave, why wallow in rue?
If the only light you see is heralded by the hope of death,
Then maybe it is time to finally succumb to the night,
Maybe, it is time to leave, and to at last seek refuge in that death.

Unlikely Lover

In you I sought an unlikely lover,
In this city of many a tower;

Of waltzes past dusk and hapless humming,
We made the mishap of dancing;

In haste we stood, speeding with no route,
We crossed the factory of love barefoot;

Ours was a fire lit by hasty amour,
And, like rain, our tears will inevitably pour;

Yet with you I'll lie, with you I'll cry,
And with you I'll finally die,
In the coffin lain,
Our sanity slain,
We'll venture together into the mist,
For we are two souls that won't be missed.

In Perdition

Still many a smile will there be,
It doesn't matter whether you leave or stay,
A child's play will still be happy,
When they you beneath the ground lay;
Can I not all my troubles just flee?
They'll all forget by day anyway,

Another Dying Man

This is one of the first dozen poems I wrote!
I had to leave it in here to honor my 12-year old self
The noose around his neck fastened,
And as his breath struggled to slip through,
His consciousness started to waver;
He saw himself at seven,
His last few days of true joy,
And then at eleven,
Standing over his father's casket;
A morbid fog rose before him,
And towards the sultry air he went,
It was the end-or was it truly?
What's to say it wasn't the beginning?
The mist took him in a daunting embrace,
And he saw himself at seventeen,
Upon his wrists scarlet slits,
At 30, he saw, his life had been asinine,
Just another of menial work and misery;
He came out of the fog,
And before him was nothing more,
No more plight, nothing to pity,
Just blackness forever, the bliss of death,
He moved no more.

The Dance of Life

Why don't you dance with me today?
We'll all soon die anyway,
It might even be the very next day,
Next week your body may start to decay;

So a dance, today, what do you say?
A dance while we can, I'll lead the way!
Forget of life, of death, that's all gray,
This is a dance of life, if you may.

Titans

"Titans! Titans! Titans galore!"
A yell rang through the hapless skies,
"Titans! Titans, and, oh, they roar!"
Of giants and of titans he cries;

"Titans!" He then bellows, again,
And our hearts do now a bit tense,
We hear them come, our spirits drain,
We shivered and we trembled hence;

Soils they tremor, and we do too,
In dread we cry, curvet, and dive,
The young clamor, and we do too,
"No! The titans will soon arrive."

Then, greater than gods, dreadful as dreams,
They came, with heads that block the sun,
I hear them all around me scream,
"Be brave! No, stay! Really? Oh, run!"

"Oh, such horror! My, what a sight!"
From east, and they eclipse the earth!
The air, fusty, be heavy with fright,
In fear we do forget our worth,

Like thin paper be crushed our will,
Warriors, peasants, they all do flee,
"The giants! Titans! They will us kill!"
Veneers shred, dread be all you see,

One by panicked one we all fall,
In death stripped of our shame and pride,
The titans, brave, are all enthralled
As this new world of blood they ride.

The Widow

A widow she is, walking in gray,
Nimble gloom's blade in the silence she strays,
Desolate her dwellings, her life did death fray,
Curtains her drawn to the misery she lays;
A curious one questions, "What happened that night?"
A rose's red paled to the shade of blood's sheen,
The white that once was be now scarlet might,
"Tell me, that night, what had it been?"
"Oh, fret not," they said, and fret not they say,
A maundering man was caught up in fate's mess,
A goblet too full, and doom's tax he pay,
A mistake, no more, and a mistake, no less;
But a killer was born, on that night just one,
And drunken she not, but sunk in malice,
With the thrust of her knife his life she had won,
And his blood, it filled none but the widow's chalice

The Soldier

Gathered a mother her months morose,
In a land with many a beach,
The isle, her home, had won a loss,
Of men, under war's long reach;
Ceaseless, she eases never her eyes,
From the waves that took her boy,
Nay straying but staying at the soughing sighs,
Of the waves that took her boy;
Sailing, he's sailing, sailing to her here,
She hopes of him on the sands,
But he was not alive, I fear,
Rather a skeleton sunk in wet sands;
Past the wash of day for two blue years,
Soldiers stepped back on the lands,
And still not she hears, not she hears,
Of the one she had held in her hands;
The cruel coast consoled with wind,
Her hopeless, haunting helplessness,
Why must he suffer? He's never sinned,
Yet the sun stole him, heading to the west;
It's by the thirtieth month she's brought,
Some vestige of him of her born,
In hands of a man be his blade, self-wrought,
From battle very much worn;
As it turns, the mother, she's killed,
By the blade her son did proudly wield,
And by her own hands she's killed,
At finding not hope's hallowed shield;
He's lost in sea, she's buried in soil,

But they saw in death a similar sight,
Each other together, in glee or toil,
Before the heist of the war, of fight.

The Butterfly

From the cocoon I came, cunning and crowned,
Now the sand I scrape, with many a wound;
Resplendent wings, wonder they found,
Now wither they pale, with none around;
The winter chill, it worsens still,
Unblessed by the grace of embrace,
Hallowing me none but a destitute's will,
Million a mask on my maundering face;
At this age where I fancy dreams not drink,
With alacrity for the end I brace,
And anticipation I find upon death's brink,
With the ones I adored now merely missed;
All my lovers are limned in languid ink,
As I wait to be by oblivion kissed,
Singing sonnets of a sorrow so pink,
My youth be just, for fond fantasies, grist.

Moments

Counting in days, your life is bleak and gray,
Recalling moments, it feels but great a boon,
You feel rue at each of your banal days,
Minutes, but some, feel they as bright as moon;
Remember your life through moments that shine,
Be they the winds of barren land of life,
Be sweetness they in holy life's sour wine,
A second may be tip of time's long knife;
In your death bed find joy at times of mirth,
In peril beam at hours that knew no plight,
Let not the drab define your being's gold worth,
And dance to hymns of yours that sing of light;
In your life past some meaning find, not blue,
And sigh as bliss drowns you in death's cool dew.

The Flower

Your petals fall to the ground you from rise,
Wilting in you what you vaunted once,
Bleak be your sense, death's blight in you lies,
Somber is your sight, with sorrowful eyes;
The verdure of joy wilts in your drought,
Sunless with clouds, but blest not by rain,
You burned your youth, as misery you wrought,
Only a sliver of bliss eking in you in vain;
All that's now gray, had been once white,
Callous, your soil is calling gloom thither,
The sky of your being hungers some light,
As in surfeit of silence, you wait till you wither,
And in this state you weave no protest nor fight:
The ending be trivial to that you find hither.

Mediocrity

The flames of your youth dimmed at mediocrity,
The shyest of your strides were striving for stars;
But now, in December, with aching molars,
Your rheumy eyes see none but mediocrity;
A father, a son, a worker, none fun,
Killed you the world you once longed to own;
In the seconds that pass, becomes your name less known,
Crippled you a country you once but could run;
You clutch to death the dreams you once wrought,
Buried in soil be what once let you blossom;
All you once coveted be tied to your bosom,
A faraway spring in the land of your drought;
In your teenage days, you flinched at mediocrity,
Roaring at the world, so wild, as a child;
But now, in your chair, your grip mere and mild,
You lie in the sun, drenched in mediocrity.

Ink and Quills

With quills may I lance our veils of pride?
With parchment may I our vices hide?

We are a race of asinine vanity,
A species of sin and crime are we;

Why must we our ephemeral lives waste?
Why must we grief inflict and taste?

All women and men who come to perish,
Poison the lands they're lain in with anguish;

I do not have a blade, but ink and paper,
And in words I shall limn a world that's better,
In words I shall paint a land with no flaw,
In words that will never any blood draw,

Hear me or not, I shan't stop,
I shall never my quill for a knife drop,
Instead, in words I will mourn those who die,
Until I, too, beneath the soil lie.

As I Lie Bleeding

I lie right now dying, I lie bleeding,
And this may one day the heavens testify;

Graces! I lie, under the sky, I lie dying,
Bleeding, my wound no man shall tend;
This stained soil on which I am lying,
Has been marred by blood for years on end;

Around me is war, the playground of Ares,
We worship the morbid, and pray to our greed,
Every man, and soul, this war harries,
Of all our morals may we bleed;

Here is a blade, and here a babe's blood,
Here is a flame, and rage I mayn't tame,
We are the wicked, the cunning, and crude,
We are the ones who each other fain maim;

We stab, we stalwart, fight, and feign,
We pare to be princes, queens, a king,
We do, for ourselves, for our kin, in this reign,
Is it not, alas, but a vain, asinine thing?

What is it all for? For what, any way?
What may my death in the end summon?
What shall I have? In tribute a day?
An effigy of bronze, of gold, of iron?

I give up my life, my blood feeds the soil,

I die, and I'm cold and covered in lather,
Why? I die for my kin, to soothe toil,
I die for my kind, for the joy of another:

I die so that we may thrive, may strive,
I die to sever these tethers of our pain,
I die, I die, so that peace may arrive,
I die, please, may not it be in vain;

I am indeed, dying for you,
I die now, and I would die thrice,
I would, bleed and die anew,
For you, and even your smile would suffice;

I lived for the good, I lived for the great,
And as I lie bleeding, I do for it die,
Oh, may our deaths our avarice sate,
In such hopes do I bid you goodbye.

The House

To the crow's dying croak,
And the clang of the silver lock,
The house stood still,
With a body of brick and rock;

To the willow's worried whisper,
And the clouds' crying cover,
The house stood still,
With chairs of faded leather;

To a hanging body's sway,
And the mist's mournful gray,
The house stood still,
Haven for ghosts astray.

The Boy Who Died

*I think, if I were behooved to pick
a favorite, I'd pick this one*

Oh, did you hear that tale of old,
Of that young boy who died?
He was only eight, with hair of gold,
And ruddy cheeks that have now dried;

His cadaver lies in the cemetery,
Beneath the moist brown soil he be,
Under the stooping apple tree,
Bearing fruit he shall not see;

Hear this tale, and hear it well,
Of this boy, with eyes of blue,
You'll hear another soon, I can tell,
From another voice with lilt of rue;

And who is he? What do we know him for?
As a rotting corpse? For his early death?
That boy, he was, but, much, much more,
And would be more, could he still breathe;

What are we, then? Our deaths merely?
Or the sum of our words, our loves, our sins?
Are we, indeed, limp corpses only?
Or limned by our vices and wins?

We are not what we leave behind,
But what we do when we do stay,

Not sinew, skin, and dead a mind,
But what we do every other day;

So hear this tale, and hear it well,
One day it shall be of you,
Of every one you've loved, as well,
Just like this boy with eyes of blue;

Think of him, as you bestow a wreath,
He had hair of gold and eyes of blue,
He was a lot more than his death,
He was, indeed, just like you.

The Funeral

I amble in the crowd by the hearse,
And all things are black or bland gray,
Veiled by clouds, the sun at us leers,
Oh why can't it be a bit gay?
Gay, for that man is rid of us,
Of shallow souls and frowning faces,
At last, he's free, not stalled by us,
He rises to a land of simple graces.

xxx

Whether this book made you laugh or cry,
I'm glad you've read, and love you for it!
On that note, I thank you and bid you goodbye.
Cleo:)

Free Space!

Manufactured by Amazon.ca
Acheson, AB